Going to the Hill is a celebration of Scotland's rich sporting heritage. Amidst a backdrop of glorious landscape from Orkney to the Borders, the photographs capture the unique world of estate owners and staff, keepers, ghillies and guests. They explore with insight and humour stalking, fishing, shooting, dog trialling and a myriad of estate activities, and give us a glimpse of life inside Sporting lodges, both traditional and modern.

Glyn Satterley is a renowned freelance photographer whose work has been exhibited widely. This is his tenth book, and his work has appeared in many magazines and newspapers, most notably *The Sunday Times, The Observer, The Independent, The Daily Telegraph, Country Life, The Field, Shooting Times, Country Living, Field Sports, Shooting Gazette, Scottish Sporting Gazette, Whisky Magazine, Golf Monthly* and *Today's Golfer*. He has spent many years documenting life on Scotland's Sporting Estates, and his earlier book, *The Highland Game* which concentrated purely on Highland Estates was published in 1992. This new book brings estate life up to the present and covers the whole of Scotland. A very versatile photographer, Glyn is best known for his work on Scottish Golf, Whisky, Hunting, Shooting, Fishing and his evocative black and white landscapes.

Going to the Hill

—— LIFE ON ——
SCOTTISH SPORTING ESTATES

Glyn Satterley

Quiller

Dedication

I would like to dedicate this book to two irreplaceable people. Colin Syrett, a great friend, who loved going to the hill, and my wife Andrea, who has supported me through thick and thin, and woven her magic both with words and pictures.

Copyright © 2012 Glyn Satterley

First published in the UK in 2012 by Quiller,
an imprint of Quiller Publishing Ltd

British Library Cataloguing-in-Publication Data
A catalogue record for this book is available from the British Library

ISBN 978 1 84689 118 2

The right of Glyn Satterley to be identified as the author of this work has been asserted in accordance with the Copyright, Design and Patent Act 1988

Designed by Glyn Satterley and Paul Saunders

Printed in China

Quiller

An imprint of Quiller Publishing Ltd
Wykey House, Wykey, Shrewsbury, SY4 1JA
Tel: 01939 261616 Fax: 01939 261606
E-mail: info@quillerbooks.com
Website: www.countrybooksdirect.com

Contents

The Sponsors

Without the generous support of the sponsors, *Going to the Hill* would most probably
have 'gone to the wall'! Their enthusiasm for the project has been tremendous, even to the
point of skippering me on a wild boat ride to 'snap' some leaping dolphins. I particularly
appreciate the wonderful hospitality, and the time you have given me, often without the
gem of a photo I had anticipated actually materialising.

 Thank you all so much.

Ronald and Erica Munro Ferguson, Novar Estate, Ross-shire

Tim Radford, Benmore Estate, Isle of Mull

Iain and Janet Wotherspoon, Glenlyon Estate, Aberfeldy, Perthshire

Arthur Irving, St John, New Brunswick, Canada

Glencalvie Estate, by Ardgay, Sutherland

Finally I'd like to mention George Goldsmith, who helped get this project off the
ground. Both George and his business partner Richard Seaman have worked tirelessly
with me, geeing me up, giving me loads of ideas, and helping get publicity and
sponsorship. A massive thanks to you both.

GOLDSMITH&CO.
CHARTERED SURVEYORS & ESTATE AGENTS

Acknowledgements

Firstly, I would like to give a huge thanks to Sir Michael Wigan, for his excellent introductory essay. He has long been an immense source of help and inspiration to me, and his pearls of wisdom have been invaluable throughout this project.

Virtually all of the photographs in the book depend upon the people in them, so their participation and cooperation, whether knowingly or not, is much appreciated.

I am indebted to the contribution made by all the keepers, stalkers, ghillies and pony boys, etc. who have accompanied and looked after me on the hill. Those who deserve a particular mention are: Peter Fraser of Invercauld, Lea McNally of Glenquoich, John Cameron of Kingie, Colin Adamson of Burncastle, Dougie MacDonald of Shiel Bridge, Neilson, Donald and Andrew of Benmore, Roland, Sam and Megan of Novar, Andrew Sutherland of Glencalvie, Gary Wright of The Hopes, David Allison, Ian Morrison, Derek Gill and Peter Allen of Reay Forest, Steve Andrews of Whitehouse, Robbie Cowan of Caerlaverock, Ronnie Buchan late of Affric, Drew Ainslie of Byrescluegh, Rab Clark, David Lisset and Derek Goodwin of Buccleuch Estates, Johnnie Hardy of the Helmsdale, Wilson Young both Senior and Junior, Bob Clark and all the team at Eskdale Shooting Services, Toby Fichtner-Irvine and Mary MacEwan and all the Islanders of the Isle of Muck, Scott Brown and team of Islay Estates, Andy Malcolm of Invermark, George Cooper and Jeff Watts of Assynt, Peter Quail of the Helmsdale, Willy Inglis of Islay and last but not least Niall Leveson Gower of North Uist.

Over the years it has taken to assemble these pictures I have been given tremendous help and cooperation from many estate owners. I would like to give particular thanks to: Ralph Percy (The Duke of Northumberland), Fergus Granville of North Uist, Sarah Holman of Shiel Bridge, Stephen Gibb of Dougarie, The Earl of Dalhousie, Andrew Gordon of Glenquoich, Scott Brown and Linda Campbell of Kingie, Ian Scarr-Hall of Amhunnsuidhe, Caroline Mann of Barisdale and Andy and Jackie Hibbert, Loch Assynt. They were all extremely generous with their time, giving me invaluable suggestions and generous hospitality, for which I am very grateful.

Sincere thanks must also go to some people who, in many different ways, helped this book come to fruition. Julia Wigan, Ian and Claire MacGillivray, Graham and Lorna Sawyer, Jon Kean, Richard MacNicol, Johnny Scott, Michael and Hilary Thomson, Bumble, David and Helen Profumo, Felix Appelbe and Lisa Bolgar Smith, James and Grace Tyser, George MacDonald, Dave and Nan Akhurst, Richard Cook, Dick Playfair, Rena Cameron, Martin St Quinton, Nancy Nicholson, Alex Hogg, Simon Blacket, John Beaton, David Foreman, Johnny Watson, Dougie McCue, Tom Hayes, Scott Thomson, Duncan Smeed and Alex Novell. Finally special thanks to designer Paul Saunders for his patience, not cropping the pictures and laying them out so thoughfully.

Thanks guys, you are all gems.

Foreword by Michael Wigan

If numbers were the cue, estates in Scotland are flourishing. There are more than ever. But estate agents' proclivity for describing anything that has a front drive as an estate must be resisted. Estate, in the minds of most, contain a recognisable imitation of sporting action.

Glyn Satterley knows the scene in its variability with all its eccentric foibles. He has cowered in a tub buried in Orcadian foreshore mud, waiting in the ferocious February dawn for the appearance of wildfowl at which his companion pops his gun, often aimlessly. He has trodden the bogs of Uist croftland with shooters, clambering over rusty wire fences and snapping at snipe whilst local ladies hang up their washing at the other end of the fence-line. Up dark glens, in remote lodges accessed only by boat, he has lit his evening candle to tramp the boards to his bedroom passing sporting records inscribed eerily in the panelling. His camera-action has frozen in minus 16 degrees out shooting hinds in Sutherland in January, and he has seen the almost zany delirium occasioned in otherwise normal people by extracting a salmon with a rod from a river.

So much has changed since Glyn's first book, *Highland Game*, twenty years ago. Then, the remnants of smart society were dressing formally for dinner.

New owners have brought in new ways – sometimes a pastiche of the old ways – and the old brigade has transmogrified. Estates in Scotland are owned by a diverse international assortment. New City money has tumbled in, assured individuals de-helicoptering flashing greenbacks at their fresh Caledonian amusements to the expectant delight of weather-beaten locals. There are secretive businessmen who never show face, money patriarchs from distant continents, movers and shakers wanting to move and shake less, Scottish businessmen following the form of their nineteenth century predecessors and laying down supposedly imperishable domains, devotees of safari parks, cultural soirees, music and culinary festivals, and situations where the laird hauls pots for lobsters presented later to high-rental house tenants.

Constituting the majority are the old sporting families who arrive in dirty 4x4s , dogs tumbling from a boot crammed with select drink, whose fishing rods and rifles have been in the safekeeping of the gamekeeper since last year. To them, colour-drained paint peeling in the same spot, a badly-lit staircase surmounted by a moth-eaten stag head, and the fading prints of Edwardian heroes of the hill are reassuring features, a soothing reconnection with the glens and lochs and turbulence-free quietude of the hills. Often they know more about the hills and wildlife than they readily let on. Their Scottish holiday venues have enmeshed with their lives and the lives of their children.

The latest estate proprietors are community bodies, normally trusts, whose purchases have been well-oiled with lottery funds. At first shying away from sporting activities they have tended with passing time to realise that this raison d'etre makes sense of otherwise inappropriately situated edifices and infrastructure. The necessity to generate income in a sprawling landholding where costs can burgeon uncontrollably has been a sobering experience. Traditional estate owners never did profiteer from their cumbersome landholdings, as the new community owners have discovered for themselves. Community land ownership has partly defused the criticism that a few owned a lot.

Activities? They are unaltered. How could they alter? If you see salmon splashing in the river winding down the glen what can you do but tie on the ghillies' recommended fly, containing a secret strand that makes all the difference, cast it into the stream and watch the outlandish creation come bumping round on the current? 'See the face on him', breathes the ghillie as the fish's flopping fades. I remember my son, plonked in the rowing boat as we enticed trout from the rippling loch water, turning a live fish over and over in his hand, peering down its throat in insatiable inspection.

If there are deer parading the hills, you must be near them. Only in stalking do you learn how deer behave, how watchful they are and how elegant their movements. The crashing antlers of fighting stags can shake the peat beneath you. When the antlers are prepared for mounting you see how gruesome are the skull-injuries they do to each other whilst fighting for hinds, breaking and cracking bone and piercing the skin.

Hinds are the smart set. They know you are there and it is unnerving when they look sharply up, staring in your direction without a whiff of your wind or any movement of your person. The instinct they use to detect you (primordial defences) are perhaps connected to those that in visitors reawakens an evolutionary linkage with the hills – atavistic sensations that defy accurate description.

There are as ever, the 'Issues'. deer no longer need to be thinned down and the reality is a sad shortage of deer. Icy winters in 2009 and 2010 hacked swathes from the red deer population, whilst heavy culling rolled imperturbably on. The public has awoken to the pointlessness of a landscape devoid of either sheep or deer, and conservation activists promoting wilderness for its own sake and preaching the reinstatement of a mythical land predating the Bronze Age have won over few hearts. The red deer remains to the Scottish public a mammal of almost mythic beauty and significance.

Their territory no longer stretches unimpeded from coast to coast. New fencing for forestry plantings, efforts to micromanage land by first demarcating it, and roads for wind farms bifurcating ranges of hills have split the landmass into smaller parcels. Deer have learned to occupy the niches. The days of seeing a party of 800 stags steadily traversing a Sutherland hillside against a receding backdrop of hazy hills, browsing as they went, an Africa-scale spectacle, are gone. July stags still aggregate and wander, but those big roving herds are broken up now.

The top-dollar sport of grouse shooting has been ramped up higher. Whilst previously, owners were plagued by the cyclical nature of populations, moving from years of abundance to disease outbreaks decimating the grouse stock, momentarily it appears that parasite treatment in grouse (by medicating their grit, and if necessary by catching them up at night and inoculating them with prophylactics) has evened out grouse cycles. There are parts of Scotland where in early morning, convoys of vehicles climb the hills to disgorge armies of beaters that march in lines moving grouse in front of them, whilst across the ridge another beater brigade is assembled to shift a different line of birds, all ensuring shooting momentum for the guns. This justifies the dizzying rents shooters pay to participate in the supreme wing-game shooting experience.

Shooters pitched to the top of their bent certainly go home with the sort of 'high' that only serious money can buy. And the profitless hills are generating wages and employment and healthy action for many people.

To provide a fitting backdrop to the vibrant house parties that bring to life a sporting estate astonishing edifices have been constructed and crumbling ones restored. Only a few have been sadly neglected. The sums of money spent on some estates by vigorous owners enraptured by the distribution of Caledonian largesse may be tittle-tattle. Beyond doubt, though, the capital sums spent on some estates has been enormous. Scotland has been blessed with muscular infrastructures which in faraway places would not be provided by any other lifestyle.

Losses? Maybe the Scottish wildcat. DNA tests reveal a legacy of feral intermixing with the original Scottish wild strain. Unlike the capercaillie, which was reintroduced from Scandinavia in the eighteenth century, the pure Scottish wildcat has no continental refuges and may be gone.

Glyn Satterley has been absorbed in this scene for a long time. He has watched both the social and physical transformations, his camera has recorded them, and he has engaged with the participants. He is capable on the estate scene of becoming part of the furniture. He is one of those people who can strike up with anyone at all, which has given him access to scenes which would normally be private. His selection is a social record; no comparable register of what has happened has been accumulated by anyone else. His humour, understanding and empathy with what is taking place shine through. As neither a fisher nor a shooter, his photographs maintain an objective edge which provides the hitting power. I have worked with him a long time, to the extent that when we talk through the issues I realise subliminally we have developed a kind of shorthand which would confuse anyone listening in!

His book, definitive of its subject, constitutes a peepshow of the leisure activities that occur in a land of fabled beauty. It is a land, too, which arouses in its admirers and its occupants a special kind of devotion.

Author's Introduction

It is amazing to think that twenty years have passed since the previous book *The Highland Game* was published, and that was twelve years in the making. So my fascination with this way of life has spanned over thirty years. Things have moved on, attitudes have changed, a few of my favourite characters have passed away and some of the lodges I explored now lie empty. *The Highland Game* carved out a niche for itself as 'an affectionate look at a lifestyle that was becoming extinct'. I made many friends 'on the hill', both estate owners and employees, and have been able to continue photographing aspects of estate life periodically since then, mainly through magazine assignments. Significant changes of late prompted me to take an in-depth look once more at what has become of that lifestyle. My close and astute friend, Michael Wigan, has kept me up to speed with how things have moved on from the perspective of landowners, politically and on the ground.

Although the bulk of photographs in *Going to the Hill* were shot over the last couple of years, some stem from 1992 when *The Highland Game* was first published. *Going to the Hill* reflects life on Scottish sporting estates throughout the whole country.

Many things have changed since my first encounter with gamekeeper Donnie McKay at Suisgill, up the Helmsdale Strath. Sadly Donnie is no longer with us, but he was my guide and inspiration, the person who opened the door to estate life for me. Anne Duchess of Westminster is also gone. She gave me invaluable support over the years, and allowed me free access to her home, Lochmore Lodge, to try and capture a way of life that was rapidly changing. Ironically, as we go to print Lochmore Lodge has had a demolition order placed on it partly because it has not been used since the mid nineties. There are positives too. Last year I went up to Reay Forest to photograph two newly-born stalking pony foals and learned that there are now more hill ponies on the estate than there have been for years. I also watched Ian Morrison, who had been stalker to Anne Duchess, help test out the new multimillion pound hydro scheme the estate had just installed.

As with the original book, it was never my intention to produce a comprehensive look at sporting estates. It is very much a personal dip into aspects of estate life that interest me, and which I have been fortunate to document. I hope it conveys a flavour of this way of life as it remains, and allows the reader to reflect a little on some of the changes that have taken place. It is an environment that I love being in, and have been fascinated to photograph over the years. I still relish the challenge of being out on the hill in the harshest of weather, and am still in awe of the dramatic and spectacular scenery. It is still an adventure to go out with keepers and stalkers on quad bikes or Argocats, and to tackle an extremely steep hillside. Visually, it almost always delivers something, whether it involves being in a boat cruising around small islands spying deer, catching grouse in a net on a freezing moonlit night or following a keeper whistling pheasants up a hillside. The ambience of the lodges is unique; each has its own routine and tradition. I am talking, of course, about the food, the drink, the afternoon tea, the time to relax, the getting ready to go, the morning meet, the going to the hill or river, the action and the dinners. For me, above all else it is the people you share the day with – the owners, the guests, the keepers, stalkers, ghillies, pony boys, beaters and pickers-up who make the experience what it is. Without their company, guidance, reassurances and crack the experience would be an empty one.

There have been important changes of note. Some estates have been bought over for communities, and are still trying to come to terms with running it for themselves. Because of new legislation everybody now has the right to roam, though previously it was an accepted right anyway. Many estates have tried to diversify, and some lodges host cookery courses, painting or photographic workshops and offer holiday lets. Spectacular new lodges have appeared while other older ones struggle to survive, and even some of the grandest sporting lodges can now be rented for certain weeks through the season. For me the most alarming change is the way the public's perception of deer has been 'transformed' into thinking they have become like vermin, and that trees should have priority over them. I meet a great number of tourists through my work whose prime reason for coming to Scotland is to see wild deer. A number of years ago I produced a book called *Trustlands* (looking at National Trust for Scotland properties). In it I had to be very careful about bringing in the prickly subject of why deer had to be culled on NTS properties. I sought the help of Lea MacNally Snr to gently explain that deer had no natural predators and culling was essential to the well being of the herds. Today the NTS openly encourages deer culling, as can be seen at Mar Lodge whose deer population has been massively depleted, in an attempt to recreate the old Caledonian forest.

Wind farms have arrived big time, amidst controversy, and as I illustrate, some estate owners have benefited and are glad to embrace them on their land, whereas for neighbouring owners they can be a thorn in the flesh, especially visually. There is also the bizarre project going on at Langholm, where keepers are employed to go out and feed harriers daily, to help stop them predating on grouse chicks. Today's trainee keepers at North Highland College in Thurso are being taught to measure and monitor habitat conditions precisely. This will become a regular work practice for all moorland keepers, and will give them a scientifically-based awareness of grazing levels, and help with habitat management. One recent change that brought a smile to my face was when I saw a stalker carefully don a pair of surgical gloves, before gralloching a deer, miles out on the hill. Health and Safety please note, he did take them off before he ate his piece!

Change is inevitable, on sporting estates as with every other industry, and it has been interesting to witness so many changes over the years. Most have been for the better, though a few, in my opinion, have not. Nevertheless, what seemed to me to be a 'lifestyle' under threat has continued to thrive and develop, amidst a backdrop of politics and the conflicting interests of estate owners and national bodies.

What has not changed significantly, and for which I am eternally grateful, is the stage on which all of this drama takes place. Our Scottish landscape remains unique and awe-inspiring. As a non-shooter I still have difficulty coming to terms with the idea of killing for sport, but I do appreciate the lure of the arena, and the uniqueness of the life it encompasses.

Donnie's Last Journey, Helmsdale, Sutherland.

Donnie McKay, who was my inspiration for my previous book *The Highland Game*, sadly died in March 2005. Having retired from keepering, he found a new lease of life as a preacher and was much sought after in churches throughout the Highlands. He also had a large following in the piping world, and his funeral was attended by people from all walks of life.

Grosvenor Estates Trustees' Meeting, Kylestrome, Sutherland, Spring 2003.
This was the last time I saw Anne Duchess of Westminster (*seated left*). She was a great helper and supporter of the last book, as well as being a star in it. She died in September 2003.

Great Stalking Country, Benmore, Isle of Mull.

The Old Bothy, Loch Stack, Reay Forest, Sutherland.
This much loved building with 'Arkle' as a backdrop has been snapped a thousand times by passing tourists, and thankfully was given a preservation order a few years ago. Ironically, as we go to print the nearby Lochmore Lodge, which featured in *The Highland Game* has just had a demolition order placed on it.

Glen Affric Lodge, Inverness-shire.
Of all Highland lodges, Glen Affric is possibly the most iconic, spectacularly set amongst some of Scotland's most beautiful and dramatic landscape.

Springtime Red Deer Herd, Mar Lodge, Braemar, Aberdeenshire.
This was a very common scene, even ten years ago, but not one that tourists are likely to enjoy
in the foreseeable future. The powers that be (Scottish National Heritage and the National
Trust for Scotland) have systematically culled the deer population around the Braemar area,
to protect trees, in an attempt to recreate the old Caledonian forest.

Heather Burning Patterns, Speyside.
Scotland's heather moorland is a unique and important
environment, without which we wouldn't have grouse.

◄ *Opposite (above and below)* **Lochdhu Lodge, Altnabreac, Caithness.**
When I took the first picture over twenty years ago, the Lodge appeared like a
mirage on the horizon as you approached it over the peat bog and heather landscape.
Now the beautiful flow country landscape has been overwhelmed by a sea of trees.

Heather Burning, Bowhill, The Borders.

Few people realise how important heather management is to grouse. Burning is done on grouse moors to regenerate plant growth and create different heights of heather to provide both shelter and food. For anyone who has been involved, it holds great nostalgia, especially the reek on your clothes and camera bag, which lingers for ages.

Heather Burning Fire Engine, Glen Almond, Perthshire.
An extravagant new variation on the old hazel broom that was once used for keeping heather fires under control. Health and safety now impose strict regulations to prevent hill fires getting out of control. In the past they have been known to travel many miles given a 'favourable' wind.

Digging for Grouse Survival, Kettleshiel, The Borders.

In December 2010 the Lammermuirs grouse moors were so heavily covered in snow the grouse couldn't access the heather they needed to survive, both for shelter and food. The majority upped and left in the hope of finding heather elsewhere, but many perished. Keepers valiantly tried to keep some areas of heather free from snow in an attempt to help their plight.

Butt Preparation, Invercauld, Aberdeenshire.
Winter weather takes its toll on outdoor structures like grouse butts, hence the need for pre-season repairs. Perched high above the Braemar road, many would envy keeper Peter Fraser his 'office'.

Feeding Deer, Glenquoich, Inverness-shire.
Lea McNally has been feeding deer through the winters at Glenquoich for
many years. As Lea arrives at each of the five feeding stations, amazingly,
the deer wait patiently for him like children for a school bus.

Putting out Grouse Grit, Invercauld, Aberdeenshire.

This activity has been carried out on many grouse moors for years. It helps birds with their digestion. However over the past ten years they have used medicated grit, which has dramatically reduced deaths from worms and other diseases. Grouse numbers are currently at a record high.

Night Time Grouse Catch-up, Burncastle, The Lammermuirs.

Another thing that is helping keep grouse numbers unusually high is the practice of catching the birds at night and drenching them with medication. Keepers are also able to keep check of worm densities in their gut by examining the caecal dropping (they do this first thing in the morning). It is almost impossible to catch the birds in daylight, and it is a bizarre activity to witness at night – men racing around with lamps on their heads brandishing butterfly nets!

Butt Decision, Burncastle, The Lammermuirs.
Most lines of butts are positioned where they are for good reason. However, head keepers and moor owners will notice subtle changes in wind direction over the years, and decide to try out new lines. Here Ralph Percy (Duke of Northumberland) and head keeper Colin Adamson discuss how the temporary wooden hurdles have performed, and whether to make them permanent sunken stone butts.

Above **Putting out Lunch for
The Langholm Harriers, Dumfriesshire.**
During the nesting season Andrew Johnstone
and other keepers at Langholm put out dead,
day-old chicks. This is part of a diversionary
feeding experiment, to curtail harriers from
predating on grouse chicks. This is part of a
bigger project Langholm Estate has been
working on with both SNH and the RSPB.

**Harrier Helping Himself to Lunch,
Langholm, Dunfriesshire.**
(Photo Copyright – Laurie Campbell)

Black Lunans Duck Feast, Whitehouse Estate, Perthshire.
Steve Andrews can literally charm the birds from the trees. He has created some unique
pheasant and duck drives at Black Lunans by the lure of food and his whistling. Like
the Pied Piper of Hamelin, he entices them up onto high ground, way above their usual
territory, in order to provide extraordinarily high birds as they fly back down to roost.

Putting out Salmon Fry, River Helmsdale, Sutherland.

The River Helmsdale is one of the most highly regarded and sought after salmon rivers in Scotland. However, the fishery board take nothing for granted and annually restock their system with large numbers of fish from their hatchery.

Left Casting a Creel, Kylestrome, Sutherland.

Stalker Peter Allen spends summer evenings checking his lobster creels in Kylestrome Bay. Often the Lodge dinner menu benefits from his catch.

Checking Grazing Densities, Sandside, Caithness.

Within the next few years this will become a regular chore for all keepers. Habitat observation, specifically highlighting overgrazing, especially by deer, will help the estate keep a check on deer numbers and give data about the area's fauna. These young keepers benefit from Thurso's North Highland College's policy, where their classroom is often out in the real world.

◄ *Opposite* **Feeding Partridges, Novar, Ross-shire.**
Megan Henderson is one of a new generation of highly qualified keepers coming through from colleges such as North Highland at Thurso.

Jimmy Unleashes The Glenlyon Hounds, Perthshire.
Universally, keepers and stalkers are obsessed with controlling
foxes and Jimmy Lambie is no exception. He does, however,
have the advantage over most other keepers who usually work
single handedly, aided only by a couple of terriers. Jimmy runs
a pack of thirteen fox hounds.

► *Opposite* **Peter Fraser,
Invercauld, Aberdeenshire.**
Peter is the doyen of Highland
keepers, a gem to be with either on
a grouse moor or out deer stalking.
It will be a sad loss to the sporting
world when he retires.

Laird of The Isle of Muck.

Lawrence McEwan is the charming Laird of Scotland's newest sporting estate, The Isle of
Muck. Shooting commercially only started about five years ago, when a few birds were
reared and 'put down'. It has now grown significantly, and along with the native wild
ducks, geese and increased numbers of reared birds, is a much sought after destination.
Lawrence does not shoot, but can be found, along with all the other residents of this
beautiful island, in the beating team.

The Ultimate Sporting Lodge, Drumlanrig Castle, Dumfriesshire.
Although Drumlanrig has traditionally been exclusively a family home to the
Dukes of Buccleuch, it is now available for sporting parties to rent.

Above **The Early Morning Swim, Sheilbridge, Ardnamurchan.**
Sarah Holman is not just content with the rigours of stalking and organizing house parties, she also regularly takes in an early morning swim, whilst the bath is running. Even though it was a chilly three degrees that day, she plunged in unperturbed.

Left **The New Arrival, Novar, Ross-shire.**

**The Cleaning Squad,
Reay Forest, Sutherland.**
These ladies were heading
for one of the outlying lodges
on the estate to prepare for
incoming guests.

Morning Cleaning, Glencalvie Lodge, Sutherland.

Corrour Lodge, Inverness-shire.
This amazing contemporary building of granite, glass and
steel is a unique contrast to the traditional highland lodge.

The Atholl Army, House of Bruar, Perthshire.

The House of Bruar created by Mark and Linda Birkbeck has become an essential part of Scotland's sporting world, particularly for clothing and food. A 'must stop-off' for many on their way North, it seems an age since the Duke of Atholl and his army came to open Bruar in 1995.

The Kit Room, Glencalvie, Sutherland.

The Morning Uplift, Floors Castle, Kelso.
Occasionally, shooting parties are able to stay at this magnificent castle.
Eskdale Shooting Services' fleet of vehicles sweep in ready to pick them
up and whisk them away to various shoots throughout the Borders.

Getting Ready for the River, Glencalvie Lodge, Sutherland.

The Morning Meet, Glenlyon, Perthshire.
There is always an air of excitement just before the guns,
guests, keepers, 'picker ups' and dogs leave for the 'pegs'.

The Ghillie's Breakfast, the Bothy, Invercauld, Aberdeenshire.
This ritual on the last day of the stags at Invercauld sees pony boys, ghillies,
stalkers, the factor, guests and even photographers having a gargantuan
feast before going to the hill.

Drawing the Pegs, The Hopes, The Lammermuirs.
Shooting guests 'draw' a number in the morning which determines which butt
or peg they will occupy throughout the day. Wilson Young, the shoot organiser,
keeps a keen eye out for any cheating.

At the Target, Benmore, Isle of Mull.

Each morning the people who are stalking go to the target. This is not just to test their proficiency, but also to test the rifle's accuracy. Interestingly, I've noticed in the last few years, even with more and more use of silencers, the observers now tend to cover their ears.

Arriving on the Hill, Invermark, Angus.

This hilltop gathering was ready for a day's walked-up grouse. No stroll in the park, the procession was led by the Earl of Dalhousie, who set an impressive pace. Younger followers and even photographers struggled to keep up with him!

The Helicopter Departs, Invercauld, Aberdeenshire.
Looking somewhat dismayed, these guns were deposited high up on the Invercauld hillside in pursuit of ptarmigan. Helicopter is not the usual mode of transport, but this was a charity auction day.

Marching to the Pegs, Bowmont Valley, The Borders.
Led by Bob Clark these loaders at Thirlestane have a military air about them!

Going to the Partridges, Drumlanrig, Dumfriesshire.

Spying, Borelick.

Going to the Hill, Rottal Style, Angus.

Estates have tried all manner of vehicles to get grouse guests to the butts. This Haglund was the most impressive I have seen. A Scandinavian ex-military vehicle, it could go anywhere but was rather cramped inside if you were carrying photographic gear.

◀ *Opposite above* **Young Beaters Hitch a Lift to the Hill, Bowmont Valley, The Borders.**

◀ *Opposite below* **Summoning Help, Reay Forest, Sutherland.**
Not a sight you want to see if you are on the hill, miles from anywhere, though generally these amazing 'go anywhere' vehicles are brilliant both summer and winter. Whatever, you certainly cannot just call the AA.

The Novar Swing Bridge, Ross-shire.
On this riverside drive, certain guns have to go to their pegs over this 'moving' bridge.
Quite a sight when being crossed by a convoy of guns, beaters and dogs.

Walking on High, Forest Lodge, Perthshire.
This was an idyllic start to the day of 'walked-up' grouse, with shafting light on spectacular hills, and a carpet of heather.

Going to the Sea Pools, North Uist.
Visually, a magical place to be – and the added bonus of some
of the best sea trout fishing anywhere.

Opening Day on the Tweed, Junction Pool, Kelso, 2011.

Looking for Stags, Assynt Foundation, Sutherland.

Assynt, like Knoydart, is one of the estates that has been taken over by a community buyout.
The lovely old lodge has been made more functional and is now available to let, to hill walkers,
bird watchers, etc. but does still cater for stalking parties. Stalking continues much as it always
has, and I went out with a couple of contract stalkers who were employed by the foundation.
No matter what your political views are, the estate landscape is some of the most dramatic and
beautiful to be found anywhere. Looking for stags, with Suilven as a backdrop, was stunning.

'Spring' Pointer and Setter Trial, Tomatin, Inverness-shire.
These Easter-time trials are often a lottery regarding the weather. This one was
brought to a halt as a snowy squall passed through, leaving the landscape covered
in white, frozen, human and doggy sculptures.

David Lisset, Buccleuch Estates, Dumfriesshire.
David, who works from the immaculate estate kennels near Durisdeer, is regarded as one of the best gundog trainers in Britain. His trophy cabinet is bulging with prizes from Field Trials across the UK. When you see him working with dogs, and often their owners, he makes solving the problem seem extemely simple and logical.

British Cocker Championships, Drumlanrig, Dumfriesshire, January 2011.
All the great and the good of the Cocker spaniel world descended on this Dumfriesshire estate over two days in January. Although extremely frosty and overcast, a good deal of the trials were run on open ground, rather than in woodland, making it a little easier to try and capture these frenetic little dogs in action.

Calling in the Geese, Caerlaverock, Dumfriesshire.

Crouched low, jammed behind a camouflage net at the crack of dawn, awaiting geese to come towards the decoys, is a really exciting experience. Will the geese come our way or not? On this occasion Robbie Cowan, the Caerlaverock keeper, successfully 'called in' passing birds by blowing the wooden goose caller.

The Shapansay Wildfowling Butts, Orkney.

From my experience, Scottish island sporting expeditions often deliver that little bit of extra magic, either from the weather, the landscape, or just getting there. Shapansay is no exception. On this occasion we were popping our heads out of sunken plastic barrels. On another morning we had been deposited on a tiny island off Shapansay, in the dark waiting for ducks and geese. As the light eventually came up we found ourselves surrounded by seal pups on the shoreline.

Above **Bringing in the Ponies, Kylestrome, Reay Forest, Sutherland.**

This peaceful procession heading back to the lodge at Kylestrome had been preceded by manic activity. It took us hours to catch and tether the ponies, and persuade them it was time to come in from their summer grazing and start their stalking duties.

Knoydart Supporters Arrive for the Handover, Inverie, March 1999.
Knoydart is among a number of sporting estates that have been purchased for the community by a mixture of government, lottery and individual funding. Some have continued to exploit sporting activities to generate income, while others have turned in other directions, such as forestry, hydro and tourism. Heralded by their supporters as 'the way forward ideologically', most of them have had problems financially. It is a fact often overlooked by idealists that many traditional estates wouldn't have survived without money being earned from 'off the ground', in the city or from industry.

◄ *Opposite, below* **Having a Break, Kylestrome, Reay Forest, Sutherland.**
Head stalker David Allison gives the ponies a break on the way back from their summer grazing. The number of stalking ponies Reay Forest has on the ground has increased. They are a brilliant sight, but sadly disappearing from a lot of estates.

The Stalking Party, Glen Affric, Inverness-shire.
On this particular day out on the hill, stalker Ronnie Buchan not only had to put up with four people in the party, but also accommodate the photographer and find a 'shootable' stag. Great stalker that he is, Ronnie delivered the goods.

The Stalkers' Companions, Glencalvie, Sutherland.
You would think dogs would be bad news when stalking, possibly barking or whimpering and giving the game away to the ever alert deer. Not so with these two black terriers belonging to stalker Andrew Sutherland, who kept right by us the whole day, never uttering a sound – even when the rifle and stalker crept in for a shot.

Sea Trout Fishing, Loch Stack, Reay Forest, Sutherland.
Loch Stack was once regarded as one of the great sea trout lochs, but sadly catches have
dwindled in recent years. Scientific studies have openly pointed the finger at fish farms
in west coast estuary waters as being the culprit. This day we didn't affect the statistics,
only managing to catch a few small brown trout.

Dapping, Loch Ba', Benmore, Isle of Mull.

Dapping is one of those absorbing activities, whether you are a fisherman or not, that really gets hold of you and drives you to perfect your technique. You simply have a rod with very light floss line and a fly at the end. Your aim is, by holding the rod out in front of you, to make the fly dance over the surface of the water in an alluring way, using the wind to keep it airborne. Loch Ba', when the wind is right, can be perfect.

The Board Walk, Glencalvie, Sutherland.
These numerous wooden walkways at Glencalvie intrigue me. Our Victorian predecessors would just not be beaten. They originally erected boardwalks on both sides of this very steep-sided section of the River Carron in order to fish every nook and cranny up to the dramatic Falls Pool.

Landing Party, Kingie, Inverness-shire.
This landing from Loch Quoich was very close to where I had landed many years before, with Alex and Farquhar Boyd, going to the hinds. The calmness was so unlike the Arctic conditions we experienced then, when the ice had to be broken before we could get across the loch.

Above **Learning from the Master! Benmore, Isle of Mull.**
Neilson, the retired head keeper at Lochmore estate, must have gutted a thousand fish on Loch Ba'. Here, a young angler learns how it is done from the master.

Sea Trout, North Uist Sea Pool.

Fishing a Sea Pool, North Uist.
It is a truly memorable experience to fish amongst such beautiful
surroundings, as the tide comes slowly in bringing the fish with it.

Above **Elevenses, Novar Estate, Ross-shire.**

Elevenses vary from estate to estate – sausages, smoked salmon, sandwiches, biscuits, etc. are accompanied by soup of all persuasions and a small 'hair of the dog' if required. Here Erica Munro Ferguson dispenses the Novar soup – which is legend! Whatever, elevenses are a must on shooting days.

The Beaters' Wagon, Islay Estates, Islay.

Rather like Dr Who's Tardis, a glimpse inside this wagon reveals it to be full to the gunwales, including one of the guns, umpteen beaters and a whole gang of dogs.

Elevenses, Out of the Rain, The Shooters' Wagon, Islay Estates, Islay.
The guns bring with them various liquid concoctions they have prepared, often over
the preceding months, such as sloe gin to both warm up their companions and to
test their constitution.

Orri Vigfusson, River Helmsdale, Sutherland.

This fantastic Icelander has single-handedly led a campaign to save the Atlantic salmon, primarily by raising huge sums of money in order to buy out virtually all the Scottish river netting stations, and also some of the coastal fishing boats. The wild Atlantic salmon has been endangered in many ways, not just by numbers taken by netting, but also from fish farming and seals. Many Scottish estates, especially those which have rights on rivers such as the Helmsdale, Navar, Thurso, Brora, Findhorn and the Spey, derive a huge part of their income from salmon fishing.

Haaf Netting, Caerverlock, River Nith, Dumfriesshire.

One type of netting not yet banned is Haaf netting, which takes place in Dumfriesshire. There are still approximately forty people who are licensed through the estate, to net the Nith. It is not for the faint-hearted – the netters line up out into the river, often up to their chests, and wait for a fish to swim into their net. All of this is done on a strong incoming tide, standing on soft gluey mud which, as I found out, gets a grip on your waders and makes it almost impossible to move. For all the effort it takes, few fish are caught by these nets today.

Pointer and Setter Trial, Tullis Hill, The Lammermuirs.
These summertime trials, with all the supporters, handlers, keepers, and masses of
pointers and setters are carried out on various moors throughout Scotland and England
for over a month. The scene is reminiscent of early Victorian sporting prints.

Athletic Setter, Tullis Hill, The Lammermuirs.

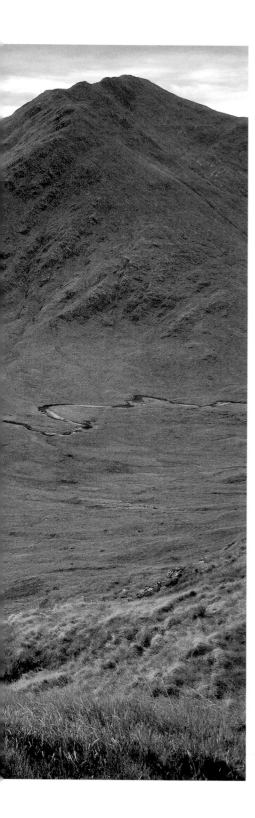

Above **The Stalk is on, Glencalvie, Sutherland.**
The body language of the stalking party reveals a lot. Here, the stalker in front has just warned that there may be a 'beast' just around the corner. They have stooped down as much as they can in an effort to not be seen, and echo the shape of the stalker.

Left **Spying The Ground, Kingie, Inverness-shire.**

Uplifting Grouse, The Hopes, The Lammermuirs.

➤ *Opposite, below* **Ralph Percy and Companion, Burncastle, The Lammermuirs.**
Ralph Percy (Duke of Northumberland) is very passionate about the moor at Burncastle and
its upkeep. Sadly, from a visual perspective, a day out amongst the beautiful Lammermuirs
landscape is about to be spoilt by the neighbouring estate who are erecting wind turbines
along the horizon.

Left **Katie Valentine (née Percy) and Italian Spinone, Burncastle, The Lammermuirs.** Ralph Percy (Duke of Northumberland) and all his family – his wife, two sons and two daughters – are all extremely good shots. I enjoyed seeing Katie Percy shooting at Burncastle, accompanied by her charismatic Italian retriever.

River Alness, Novar, Ross-shire.
This is a lovely piece of water to photograph, and produces startlingly different views around most corners. It is the classic small Highland river, and yields a good number of fish as well.

Dancing with Johnny, River Helmsdale, Sutherland.
Johnny Hardy is one of the great ghillies on Scottish salmon rivers. He works on the Helmsdale, which he knows so intimately from traversing its banks since boyhood. For inexperienced fishermen, and all ladies, Johnny takes their hand and leads them a stride further down the river, after each time they cast the fly. Even bearded 20-stone male anglers receive this treatment – no arguments. The perfect gentleman, Johnny will always avoid eye contact with the ladies, as he takes their hand.

Alert Loader and Gun, Grouse Butt, Kettleshiel, The Lammermuirs.

Wind Turbine Grouse, Farr, Tomatin, Inverness-shire.
Controversial though they may be, wind turbines have revived some estate fortunes. This one
at Farr required sixteen miles of road to be laid, which has given keepers access to the moor and
helped with vermin control. Interestingly, the highest densities of grouse are now being recorded
in and around the turbines, which probably means the blades deter raptors. It does however look
and feel a little unnatural, having huge structures whirring away in the backdrop whilst people are
shooting from butts.

Grouse in Profusion, Byerscleugh, The Lammermuirs.

Examining the Bag Before Lunch, Invermark, Angus.
There is always a fascination to examine the 'bag' as it is laid out by the
keepers before lunch, and then again at the end of the day.

Lunch!

This page and opposite

Right Isle of Muck.

Below Glen Lyon Lunch 'Hut'.

Invercauld.

Forest Lodge.
Lunch, if taken on the hill, is called your 'piece'. It is a very important part of the day; a chance to relax and take your boots off after all that walking. Essentially a drink, sandwich, and a piece of cake or fruit, the class of the piece depends on where you are staying, and whether you had to make it yourself (very common in many lodges). When stalking, the norm is also to carry your piece in your pocket, often eating it on the hoof. Stalking is arduous work and your 'piece' always tastes fantastic.

The Landing Party, Iona, (Benmore).

High summer at Benmore offers far more 'sport' than mere fishing or stalking. *Benmore Lady* can whisk you away to magical locations around the west coast. Iona, Staffa, and a myriad of other islands are on the doorstep. St Kilda is also possible. Of course when you get there you just might have to have a picnic and play rounders. Tough life!

Benmore Lady, Spotting Dolphins, off Mull.

A Bit Too Close for Comfort, Kingie, Inverness-shire.

At Kingie we were suddenly 'on a stag', and felt very exposed with nowhere to hide. But being the true professional that he is, John Cameron saved the day by leading a stealthy retreat. The stag was then approached from a different direction, and duly culled. I sympathise with stalkers who have me as extra baggage out on the hill, making it a tad more tricky to get us all close to the stag.

Fish on Demand, Junction Pool, River Tweed, Kelso.

Junction Pool, at Kelso, has become one of those great fishing Meccas, especially at the 'back end', when this piece of water is stuffed with salmon. As if trained to jump on command, a fish will pirouette into the air every few minutes with an almost monotonous regularity.

The Reluctant Loader, Aswanley, Aberdeeshire.

Left **A Cautious Look Over the Top, Glenquoich, Inverness-shire.**

The slightest adjustment in the stalker's posture, such as slowly rising up onto his tiptoes, alerts you to the fact that there just might be a stag around the corner. Some of these movements are almost balletic.

A Bit Quick Off the Mark, Glenlyon, Perthshire.
No matter how well trained some dogs are, when the pressure is on, you can
bet they'll break every rule in the book in an attempt to get that bird first –
even before it's been shot!

Crawling in, Benmore, Isle of Mull.

Most stalks involve this kind of activity. When told to do so, even if the ground
is soaking wet or happens to be black soggy peat or a burn in spate, you have to
crawl. No exception made for photographers either.

Signalling the Argo, Assynt, Sutherland.
This situation was heartening to me, to realise that out here in the wilderness even
the smartest of mobile phones and modern radios can come unstuck without a signal.
Here a supermarket plastic bag is put to a novel use as an improvised signalling device.

Releasing the Hawk, Kenmore, Perthshire.

Hawking on Scottish grouse moors has been done since Victorian times, and allows moors with low numbers of grouse to earn extra income. As a photographer, one of the problems is being in the right spot, at the right time. Often all the action – the dog on point, the falcon release, the flush of the grouse, the stoop, chase and possible kill – happens miles from where the falconer has instructed you to stand. On this occasion at the release, the peregrine flew straight at my head, giving a closer shot than anticipated.

Ducking and Diving, Novar, Ross-shire.

Rather like a boxer, a good loader will have to be alert and agile enough to avoid the swinging barrel of the gun as it tracks oncoming birds from all directions. On this lovely riverside drive at Novar, the loader has the added problem of avoiding the water.

Blooding, Kinveachy, Speyside.

This is a rather archaic ritual, inflicted on first-time stalkers, after the stag had been shot and gralloched. When this chap shot his first stag the stalker decided that the ritual should be revived. Usually a finger mark of blood suffices, but in this instance the stalker smeared his whole face. He took it in good spirits and as the day wore on obviously forgot it was there. His wife, however, was rather taken aback when she ran out to greet him on his return to the lodge.

Capturing the Scene, Shiel Bridge, Ardnamurchan.

Ian MacGillivray is considered to be the foremost contemporary painter of deer out on
the hill. He follows a long line of artists, mainly from Victorian times, like Landseer and
Wolf, who specialised in capturing the sport, wildlife and landscape of the Highlands.
Ian, I feel, differs from most other painters in that he not only draws and paints whilst on
the hill, but can frequently be found behind a rifle actually stalking, giving his paintings
an edge over others.

Hidden Gems, Loch Assynt Lodge, Sutherland.
These beautiful sporting murals, dating back to the 1870s, were uncovered whilst
renovation work was being carried out at Loch Assynt Lodge a few years ago.

Pescatorial Artworks, the Fishing Room, Amhuinnsuidhe Castle, North Harris.
It's not enough to simply catch a large fish from the wonderful array of lochs and rivers on offer at Amhuinnsuidhe. They also expect you to celebrate it by drawing, captioning and signing it on the fishing room wall.

Landing a Large Fish, Lower Birgham, River Tweed, The Borders.

Above Loading onto the
Argo, Assynt, Sutherland.

Dougie has a Fag
after the Gralloch, Shiel
Bridge, Ardnamurchan.

◁ *Opposite, below* **Examining the Gralloch, Benmore, Isle of Mull.**
Modern stalkers, overburdened by bureaucracy, are now tested on their competence
out on the hill with rifle and knife. Moreover, they also have to examine the contents
of the dead deer's stomach to ascertain if it had any ailments or diseases. I couldn't
believe my eyes when I first saw a stalker don a pair of bright blue surgical gloves
before he started to gralloch.

The 'Pony Boy', Invercauld, Aberdeenshire.
I love the expression 'pony boy', for over the years I have
seen all manner and types leading the pony back. Girls too!

Right **End of the Day, Knockando, River Spey.**
This beautiful Spey salmon ended up, one hour later, being
consumed as sushi with a glass of wine. It was fantastic.

Securing the Stag, North Uist.

Stalking on the east side of North Uist is a whole new experience, in that you spy from a boat as you motor around a series of smallish islands. The deer, particularly stags in the rut, swim from island to island in pursuit of hinds. Our trip, initially, was like a wildlife safari as we came across otters and amazingly a golden eagle sitting on a rock twenty feet away. When we finally spied our 'shootable' stag, we had to clamber over huge, slippery, seaweed-covered boulders, reminiscent of a Second World War commando raid. Once landfall was made the Stalker and the Rifle crept a fairly short distance and shot the stag. The last part was the most precarious as we had to lower the stag down a cliff face, get it over more treacherous boulders, and finally up on to the bow of the boat. Our end of day dram was well earned.

The Start of a Long Drag, Benmore, Isle of Mull.

This was a wonderful scene, set amidst such dramatic landscape, but eventually the euphoria wore off. The stag had been shot on a steep down slope, and the only way to extract it was to drag it downward, and then along the valley floor. Sounds easy, but the bottom of the valley section was a mile or two away, traversing burns every few hundred yards. The three of us shared the pulling, working two at a time, but it became more and more difficult as we got hotter and hotter, and each tiny incline felt like a mountain. The person not pulling had the added burden of carrying everybody else's discarded clothing, plus my camera kit. You can imagine our relief when we finally got it close enough for the Argo to collect it.

After the Morning's Wildfowling, Caerlaverock, Dumfriesshire.

Going Home, Invercauld, Aberdeenshire.

At the Larder, Dougarie, Isle of Arran.

Deer larders come in many shapes and sizes, but are fundamentally there to process carcasses ready for the game dealer. This one at Dougarie, built in the 1800s, goes beyond just being functional, and is aesthetically very attractive with its round frame, wooden columns and glass from floor to ceiling.

The Game Wagon, Isle of Muck.

Not sure health and safety would strictly approve of the volume of people, kids, dogs and birds this machine managed to transport from drive to drive, but it was always done in island time – leisurely and very safely.

Roland's Larder, Novar, Ross-shire.
This larder at Novar is kept in immaculate order with nothing out of place, by
Roland Van Oyen, head keeper. The birds are hung in precise order so that
counting the bag at the end of the day is quick and accurate.

Lament to the Stag, Kingie Larder, Inverness-shire.
As well as taking care of the deer carcasses, Kingie larder is the arena for stalker John Cameron to practise the pipes. A self-taught piper, John has been banished from the house by his wife Rena, so whenever he wants to practise, he seeks the sanctuary of the larder. It is common for John to entertain guests whilst the odd dram or two is taken after coming back from a stalk. Interestingly the larder acoustics are very good.

The End of a Great Day, The Hopes, The Lammermuirs.

This euphoric group of Canadians had just finished a day of driven grouse, shooting from butts for the first time. They hadn't managed to shoot many birds but this very challenging experience, set amongst the beautiful Lammermuir hills, with the heather in full bloom, had given them a real buzz. Even as a non-shooter I can fully understand their excitement, and understand why people come from all over the world to shoot in Scotland.

George Jamieson, Cramond, by Edinburgh.

It's surprising just how many deer heads, birds, fish and other animals killed during the season in Scotland are wanted as trophies, to go on the wall or sit in the office. Many more end up abroad as mementos. Taxidermists who deal with game come in many guises, mostly falling into the amateur bracket and doing it in their spare time. I've been asked to collect 'finished' heads and stuffed birds, which are poor representations of the originals. George Jamieson's work is in a different league. He has been perfecting his taxidermy skills his whole life and is a true 'artist'. His workshop, if a little macabre, is fascinating to see, filled with a menagerie of all kinds of wildlife in different stages of preservation.

Gun Room Activity, Glenlyon, Perthshire.
This 'behind the scenes' activity that few people see, is mostly carried out by
loaders or keepers. It is done soon after coming back from shooting in order
to clean and lubricate the guns.

Back from the Hill and Awaiting the Tea, Invermark Lodge, Angus.

Michel Roux at Novar, Ross-shire.

Many estates are trying to diversify these days in order to extend the season and generate more income. At Novar they had Michel Roux for a weekend, working his magic in the kitchen in the evenings. By day he was out shooting, and excelled at that as well.

Kitchen Alchemy, Glencalvie, Sutherland.

In the past, lodge kitchens were usually manned by professional cooks, invariably
women, who were there for the season. Now you are more than likely to meet a
full-blown chef. At Glencalvie I had the pleasure of snapping James Burton, who
has worked in restaurants all over the world. His food was stunning.

The Dinner Table, Barisdale, Inverness-shire.

Barisdale is one of the most charming lodges I've had the pleasure of staying in. It has no airs and graces, not at all fancy, just basic and simple. I think this picture of the dining table sums it up well with the odd chairs and the odd crack around the fireplace. Candlelit at night, you go to bed like Wee Willy Winkie, having collected your candle holder from the kitchen.

Piping in the Dinner, Kinveachy, Speyside.

The Ceilidh, Kingie Lodge, Inverness-shire.

After having had a great day on the hill, it is common at Kingie to invite stalker John Cameron and his wife Rena around for a post dinner drink, which usually turns into an impromptu ceilidh. Beware though, if reeling with Rena, her enthusiasm and ability will test even the strongest man's stamina.

The Celebration Ceilidh, Knoydart, Inverness-shire.

The day Knoydart was handed over to the community was celebrated not only by the locals,
but also by visitors, many of them musicians from far and wide. There were speeches, dancing
by children, awards, tours, tree planting and a hog roast. However, the highlight was the ceilidh
that started in the early evening and was attended by all ages. Drink was taken and I left about
1am to get some sleep in order to get the community boat back to Mallaig in the morning.
I gather that the dancing continued after the sun had come up, and on the boat going back
the musicians continued to play for the whole journey to Mallaig.

Wintering Geese, Kettleshiel, The Lammermuirs.

The Evening Duck Flighting Party, The Hopes, The Lammermuirs.

These little expeditions are carried out after the main shooting of the day has finished. Always enthusiastic for more action, some of the guns don warm kit, and led by the keeper, head off to some obscure pond in the gathering darkness. Quickly put into position around the water, huddling behind rushes, you are told to note where the other shooters are and keep quiet. There you wait until it is virtually dark. Suddenly there are whooshes, swishes and whistles as ducks begin to fly over the pond. A confusion ensues as guns go off, then silence as the ducks try to come in again. I was glad when it was all over. It became impossible to see what you were doing, the auto focus on the camera wouldn't work and my flash didn't exactly endear me to the shooters.

Winter Shoot, Thirlestane, The Borders.
In recent winters we have had some of the heaviest snow in years. This January shoot,
with a French party at Thirlestane, looked more like the Alps than the Borders.

Keepers on the Piste, Thirlestane, The Borders.
These keepers and their dogs looked fantastic as they improvised a sort
of skiing motion to get down the hill at the end of a drive.

The Last Day at the Stags (18 October), Invercauld, Aberdeenshire.

It was rather unseasonable on the last day of the stags that year at Invercauld. We had set off in the old Land Rover and Peter Fraser, the stalker, slowly drove us up to nearly 3000 feet, onto a Cairngorm snowfield. Undaunted, off we set on foot as if we were taking a Sunday stroll. No one, not even the two terriers that were with us, appeared to mind in the slightest. We did eventually come down below the snow level, and a stag was shot down in the Glen.

➤ *Opposite* **Burdened Picker-up, Thirlestane, The Borders.**

At the Hinds, Borrobol, Sutherland, December 2009.

December 2009 was one of the coldest on record. On the day I went out with Michael Wigan to the hinds, it was minus 16 degrees at lunchtime. We had donned white suits, to help camouflage us against the sheer white, frozen landscape. I had not experienced anything quite like it before. We set off up the hill and within a short distance we were trudging in snow, which was above our knees. Luckily we soon came upon a group of hinds, their darkish silhouettes making them stand out. Michael managed to sculpt out a hollow from which to lie and shoot, and very quickly one hind was dead. He managed to kill a second hind half an hour later, and we dragged them to the vehicle as quickly as possible. An urgency had crept into our actions as the cold began to bite. I do remember Michael still gave me the time to 'pose' for a few shots whilst gralloching in that frozen landscape.

Playing Dead – Not Even a Quiver, Kylestrome Deer Calf.
This courageous deer calf didn't move at all – even with my shutter
clicking from close range. I cannot help but wonder what the future
has in store for this young character out on the hill.